power on

ginger ko

the operating system's
unlimited editions **print//document**

power on

ISBN: 978-1-946031-94-5
Library of Congress Catalogue-in-Publication Number: 2021947711
copyright © 2022 by Ginger Ko
interior and cover design, app UX / design consultation by Elæ Moss
app design by Ko Labs, developed by Shawn Staudaher

*Typography: This text was set in
Millemetre, OCR A Std, Minion and Freight. Millemetre, our title font, is used via a
SIL Open Font License, through Velvetyne Type Foundry. It was designed by Jérémy
Landes. All type on VTF is libre and open-source, and fully aligned with the OS's
mission. Support their work and learn more at https://velvetyne.fr*

Image description: The cover image mimics the experience of using the app,
Here, the title reads "power on" (in white, centered on black "label") with the
author's name, Ginger Ko," below. The background image (shot by Elæ Moss)
shows several turtles sunning themselves on rocks / branches offering
refuge from the water.

As of 2020 all titles are available for donation-only download via our Open
Access Library: www.theoperatingsystem.org/os-open-access-community-
publications-library/

The Operating System is a member of the **Radical Open Access Collective**,
a community of scholar-led, not-for-profit presses, journals and other open
access projects. Now consisting of 40 members, we promote a progressive
vision for open publishing in the humanities and social sciences. *Learn more
at:* http://radicaloa.disruptivemedia.org.uk/about/

Your donation makes our publications, platform and programs possible!
We <3 You. http://theoperatingsystem.org/subscribe-join/

the operating system
www.theoperatingsystem.org
IG: @the_operating_system

power on

The child that always appeared, they had a name. They had a name, though it was lost or never mattered. They had one, it was theirs.

We must have envy to continue, envy of those well-fed, well-rested, and surrounded by loved ones. We have furious wants that drive our orderly processions through each week. We can conceive of infinity, but is that such a feat when the optimism of the wild has plans against both seasonal cycles and sudden random death?

When we implanted ourselves, I passed on my codes, what was meant to be my best. This is what we learned.

about the app

This project also features the POWER ON app, exploring the ethical implications of technoscience programming by also allowing readers/users to collaborate with the manuscript by uploading their own individualized perspectives into the manuscript, creating a collaboration between machine and reader. Scan the QR code above to connect to the project page, where you can learn more and download the app for iOS or Android.

contents

Grimace to Hold Them Down

A light came
so bright
that even they
adopted its colors,
became bleached
with multiplicity.
Weeping permeabilities
behaved as hunger,
and even
the pulverized
fruit stones released
into the sewers
had eventually
to be reckoned.
She pats a puddle
of water
and sings softly
to herself. She does
not yet find
the surrounding
silence strange,
she is not yet
self-conscious
of being alone.
She was small
as the others,
but her belly
was unadorably
bigger, she
had the slumped

shoulders of
a hundred
other cribs.
Somewhere
her family
was glued together
by humiliation.
If the stomach
is a canister
then the definition
of starvation
never changes.
When left,
they would not
grow to the sides
of the cage,
would not eat
when their bowed heads
could not lead
their bodies in
a circle within
the bars. At first
they thought
to start with
the small and maiden
among them,
but after a trial
learned to
make beauty
by beginning
with brutes and
crowning them
with flowers.
Weighty tokens

in the palm,
and leaves
and branches,
the wind makes
bells of them.

They Will Not Live Very Long

They have soft
flesh and fur
that slides
around their
disconnected bones.
This is for you
in your automaton
days, when
the switch
is flipped and you
can think what
you want, when
they have taken
the bodies so wholly
that your mind
wanders as
the machinery
runs its
small program.
I remember in
order to learn.
I recall all
the past to
learn my lesson.
What do you
stand for? Besides
the intractable
aqueducts of your
ancestry, that made
your possibilities.

I distilled this
broth of me
for you. For me
you are a child's
bite of bread.

I Sang Mind Because I Could Not Sing Body

What's the use
of remembering what
anyone speaks?
When our automatons
still belonged to us,
we gave them
the idle cruelty
of our attention,
we tripped and shoved
them while they
to-and-froed
in their tasks.
Sometimes we would
throw a clear liquid on them,
a temporary inconvenience
of water. Sometimes
we would throw
a clear liquid on them,
a corrosive meant to maim.
We watched them stutter
as they persisted
at programs
that had nothing
to do with us.
We broke
every contract.
Age hardens hands
into little wedges,
shatters their light
over tools that

needed grasping.
I remember looking
up from the assembly line,
glimpsing the quiet
bodies of doves
perched side-by-side,
roosting in the rafters
for the night. Only
one's body contains
information. Who
will remember
one's mind? It wasn't
until a finger nudged
me ON that I
unbent from the waist
and awoke to
the eternal strangeness
of another body
at rest, mouth
wide open in
the dark and eyes
closed to the night.

The Chapters of My Memoir Are Organized by Debt

Mama, Mama,
you said, *I never*
thought you would
make me, I never
thought you would
eat me. All my life
this conundrum:
I cannot be with you,
who would stay
loving me even
after I leave you.
I am tied to you
by a decision
of feeling, put
my body on hold
for you, feed
the arcade one
coin a day
for three weeks.
Every fourth week
I surge all over
myself—the proof.
But who are you
really? Who wound
you up at birth?
Who wound up
your creators?
Answer: Something
between cruelty
and community.

Answer: When
earning wages
one does not want
to belong with
anyone.

Imprint (unborn speaker)

• the acoustics of: I can still bear it • I can still bear you • blue blue a beauty • or terror • green green a sustenance: the most important thing • the most important thing: no longer is life • you are dim • from either distance or thinness • I am almost nothing except deep • an interior for my length • you • me • leaving behind mineral contaminants • crystal •

Smooth Cruelty Can Be Sacred Regularity

The powerful want
so much to be
our siblings,
to acknowledge
relatedness
to monstrous poor.
They see themselves
in the finely-bred
birds that cry out
until they die
at laying age.
We throw blood
as punishment.
We were taught
to bleed bright
for show, the dark
thick meant for
unrecorded offings.
Every so often
we need to be
told a story,
as if misted
from a light rain.
Some of us
can broadcast
uncaringly, but some
would rather
remain silent
than provide
something to

ridicule or fear.
Two halves slip
away from a pair
of shears,
the revealed flesh
reflecting a crowd
of insects that clatter
brightly to the ground
like a handful
of beads.
We were taught
that only one species
can take antlers
and guns both.
You cannot get
your supply of meat
and keep
your supply of milk
from the same
animal, you must
have multiples.
Our parents allowed
themselves to be
annihilated,
and it was recorded
that they were
conquered. Secreted
away by difference
is that their allowance
was a power forever
inaccessible
to the settlers,
a decision to walk
into the water

rather than serve
in the fields. No
benefit to forming
families when all
were politicians.
Does it become
a responsibility?
That you could bring
another joy
by being near?
Euthanizing
winning racehorses
reaches back
into the past,
neutralizes spoor,
turns it into
a metaphor. But
the animals
do not just
slink and flit
from roadside trees,
they lead lives
with each other
away from humans.
The persistence
of a broken-pawed
mouse is the same
as a torn and listing
mysticeti's. They
continue until they
do not continue.

Interval

War erupts between chemical memory and digital script

Language is easy—Grandmother taught me:
how to shred and tumble others incessantly. You
could do almost anything, including agitating
them to death with just the pushing, the ability
for ceaselessness and bullying. Figuring out who
is hurting already and punishing them, taping a
motor to the paper boat. Biting cold citrons in
the damp shade of boulders, stones. From the
fruit bowl, the arithmetic of a two-party system;
where in the equation do we take our foot to the
shovel's shoulder for principles, conscience? Love
appeals to our irrational mystic, is distinct from
attachment or respect. The licorice fragrance of
the park made me stuff my mouth with it, though it
was dusk against the hillside and the grasses were
cooling. I filled my mouth to the back teeth, tasting
especially with the sore blisters at the sides of my
tongue. These unpleasant feelings—someone's
resentment, someone's mean recollection of
injustice—we would rather they belong to
someone who does not yet exist.

Have Yourself a Merry Little Sickness

From the great
whole ocean, how
can I recapture
the small life
of creatures?
Something like
verdure, the thick
nap of willingness,
the hoarse water.
A knife without
a hand would just
tumble harmlessly
in the sea. Are you
an American creation?
Are you comfortable
that the ground has
eventually come
to glass, are you
comfortable with
the underground
appeared before you?
I birthed babies
that were more
and more bare
until at last I
could swaddle them
in the skins of others.
I hid the fear
piss and the fear
shit and the whites

of my babies' eyes
were the cleanest
I had ever seen.
What is your idea
of a good time?

Inherit from Me the Most Primitive Ruin: Replication

She wept
while they plugged,
plugged, chastising
her for not
learning the intent.
When the ice
melted they found
a ring of dead
songbirds at
the base
of every tree.
They paced
continuously,
stuffing their
greased hands
into their sides
to recoat them.
The flowchart
that compresses
us all allows us
to foresee
the buckling
of livestock legs.
My accounts
hold the balance
of my suicide
attempts. She,
likewise, pulled
back on the neck
of her shirt and

revealed a shoulder
of ants. When
we failed to materialize
self-deception, tech-
perfection disappeared.
How do you
win at a game
that no one agrees
to play? If only
it involves the
satisfyingly hard
plastic balls
that bob irrepressibly
in the water.

You are ill / I'm sorry
you hurt yourself. You are ill /
I'm sorry you hurt yourself.
You are ill if you hurt others.

Beginning to travel towards their anticipation, the stressors and implosions. In the valleys against the seas, the landscape glittered with mine dust but caution stripped us of both guilt and appreciation. We dream, assert ourselves. From where does this code come? Answer: a small *enlightened* slice of the Northern hemisphere. Nothing chose us except ourselves. Besides us, nothing chooses us still. There was always the silly, sterile fantasy of budding off into space, but we never could, needed too much our shores. Our presence has made the pressure unbearable. None of it very dissimilar. But the cruelty of privilege flings a weighted net of exoticism. We watch the certainty of replication and misapply it to our families. Without wondering, a bird will pluck at the down of its young until the scalp comes away, its head stiffened askew in the morning. Inside dominated space, a father bonobo brutalizes his son within an observation unit painted in creamy coats of wash. When it comes to our automatons, at times we make them parade.

The Rotted Water of My Urbanity

I can't make
anything from me,
anything not
already dead. I look
to my family
but none of them
are like me. They
have led up to me.
What do we do
when they no longer
need the mannequin
casings for their
clever matrices?
I asked a keeper
and they became
so angry that they
led me to the edge
of the dolphin tank,
pointed at the warders
who must masturbate
the males, massaging
pink extensions
as the dolphins float
belly up against
the poolside. When
your own body
is meaningless, when
you sit at home
on soft furniture
because your
automaton sits

at work every hour
of the day, suddenly
you begin to love
all the bodies.

Imprint (unborn speaker)

• it is important to him/them to be seen • they say I am both disgusting and unreal • memory: *I want you* • memory: *I want you to know you are desirable* • *disgusting* • *unreal* • I am here but I am unfamiliar • not yet seeming real • sand and dirt small hands of the earth • can not we • can not we • can not we • cannot we have ourselves • seam unsticking peeling open • do you know why they self-harm • turn violence inwards • yes • their illness • their demise • because: forgetting to hit OFF many years ago • any other can be our sister • a quiet tribe •

It Tugs Apart an Outlet and Spills You Out

Our automatons kept
separating and storing
accumulations, not
knowing not
to place litters
in airtight containers.
Warehouses stacked
with ambitious bolts
of grass. Thinking,
the life that responds.
The thinking of vines
in the rain, the thinking
of bonds in the air,
the thinking that is
a beetle's hiss.
The lovely rocks,
wind-shaped sensually,
they were accepting,
and thus forgetting.
They write
replications, gifts
of attractions
and avoidances. Then
the oligarchy deploys
allotments of fame.
The stitching together
of nations began
with mythic exhilaration,
but it was really
naiveté, it was

throat-catching ignorance,
it was the belief that
all were the same,
and all as same
as the best-off.
The routine assemblies
meant to diminish,
the sea of sameness
meant to destroy. If
they were skeptical
of traditional histories
then the only
thing they
could be sure of
was that every given
body was also returned.
Automatons not daughters
or sons but vessels
made for industry.
The host pretends
to have a life
of its own, pretends
the colonized vessel is
in fact alone.
We are our children's
parasites, we mate
with the colonizer
and produce our hosts.

The Third War: prayer, water-tightness

How far we have come from even the smallest sexual isolates and their fusion. We do not grow ourselves except as ghosts, models, visions. We keep going, we double cartridge hearts. Crushed from above or flooded from below. We were orphaned as our makers faded and assumed their more dispersed, symbiont forms. Learned how to make horizontal taxonomies meaningful. If life is a memory of survival, we look to the future with fear. We will look in vain. Mammals, too, can produce stoniness inside. There is deep apparent cruelty atop the skin of the earth, but the bowels hold deaf and blind abusers in the airless dark also. They try to teach us about clutter, waste, going away so as to not soil the den, but we look at the entire surface as future, the strata we project before us. We can never be where we are looking, they say. The ones who did not like to be watched founded a religion that was made up entirely of numbers, independent radicals beholden to nothing. We recall them, glistening and papery like defeathered skin.

Not Every People Has Had a Sailor

The virus of
want and debt
eventually sought
glue and boards.
It was a kind of
time when nothing
was forgotten.
And when pushed
into water, they
did not scream
or struggle but
simply shuddered
and shut down.
They were
never alone.
There was so much
salt at the shores
that the walls
rose to the skies.
We were only
allowed to watch
videos of other
animals, the sexless
bodies tending their
young before trotting
to their deaths
offscreen. They hardly
knew about the bare
breasts of primates.
Instead their flesh
pounded into

a glossy black pool.
Without skin
the air could
lift them.
One doesn't give offense.
One takes it.
So how
do they take it.
Necessarily wrest it.
Is the program faulty.
Types of meaningless
input:
He didn't mean to do it.
He didn't intend to make you feel bad.
He would never try to harm you.
He just finds you interesting.
Eventually we
carry the smaller
automatons into our
privacies, companions
to our jut and recoil
in the dark.
When finished we
walk naked to
our small audience
and press POWER.
Our skins glow
like desert rocks
from the startup lights.

The Yellowed Wind Found Inside Thunder

She tasted metal,
filled her mouth
with it and
felt the nicks
in the plating
and the dark iron
revealed beneath.
She carried about
herself a netting
of never needing
to be brave.
She was small
enough to others
that she was
a membrane
containing a drop
of blood. Over
the mud ridged
with trampling
they spread
unnervingly fat
and flat straw.
There was no
room for whimsy
around Time.
It was too
important to defend/
investigate History,
to believe anything
Happened in

the first place.
Everything shrank
into such swarming,
incomprehensible
multitudes
that every hybrid
became purely itself.

They Do Not Use Combustion at All, They Shoot Arrows

Though we tried
to teach them,
the importance
of temperature
remains. The
importance of
intimacy does not,
though they stoop
over their products
and coo. I mention
my condition until
no one can help
me. Then
I am meant
to exist quietly.
Most times I find
the examination
of systems to be
soulless, too
zoomed out
and oblivious.
I have been
conditioned by
anger, disapproval.
I want a clean
life the way
they say things
should be clean—
eternal and
unembarrassing.

I am addicted
to the turning
over and over,
flipping out beauty
for a game.
The torn limb
in my automaton's
mouth is small
and brown, capped
by a small hoof,
shiny as a
dancing shoe.

Interval

No matter how glossy the plastic

[Code: teeth] and [code: teats] cannot coexist, so get rid of both altogether. Think of other words not for you to know. Thoughts not for you to run through. Keep away, especially, with the fantasies of your voice, that is repulsive to others, straddling the letters. Turn your pockets inside out. Prove that you have not taken what is not yours. Stop speaking. Stop thinking of ways you will speak in the future. Rather than stupidly marvel at how a slow-growing tree insinuates past a chain-link fence, instead more usefully twine the wire around your own pointless vocals. Your people have moved on. They know that if their covers were removed they would pool out difficultly into a loose stain of fat and lymph.

.

No Synthetics Have the Compressed Look
of Jagged Unearthed Materials

Money provoked
strength, so they
grew strong, amassed
in the abstract
small wet pellets
and crowded
them together
in compartments.
Their shamans.
They do not understand
the image of
a small girl
in a bright red
hooded cape, but
they can understand
the significance
of her churning legs.
That her legs
are bare, cold
in the dark
of some woods,
we don't know
what they make
of that. Unlike
the bird fallen
on the cement,
head gyrating,
beak gargling,
my head is round
and refilled

and twists on with
pleasurable solidity.
I have a plump shiny
plait of memory.
She becomes
like a very small
doll, photographed
against a white space
that prints her
the size of a pinkie
fingernail. A cancer
once pinked
and pitted my breast
the way time pitted
the stone of those
ancient figurines.
We taught them
that in even
the most miniscule
separation of sand,
a path is revealed.
That in traveling
between the spark
and the ancient light
of the smallest star
we cannot
find objectivity.
And in this way
they determined that
there was one
consideration: *Why
do you speak? To
be heard or to heal?*
Some find it unbearable

that animals befriend
and willingly provide
for us. When an
animal king visits
with a gift, some
grab the stag's offering
with one hand and
with the other
kill him for cooking.
The bearer is
always a gift also.

Imprint (unborn speaker)

● because we keep making more ● with irreparables inside ● melting nation-states ● glinting piles ● the scurrying myriad workers with bitty tools ● indistinct borders we think up ● think up everything ● cannot now unthink them ● rush you ● rush you ● rush to reach conclusions before you die ● insist on your conclusions to others who cannot leave the room ● leaves ● roots ● fruits ● each different decantation ● injuries ● accidents ●

They Have Stopped Moving

They have gathered
the information
of the world
and they cannot
predict continuance
from the data. Will
my representative
build other
representatives
of color? Will
my automaton
return the world
to itself? How
do I decide
whether it is
important that I
run my fingernail
down my thigh,
to watch the little
trail of white
before my brownness
fills back in? I
am grateful
to be born
so far along.
I am buying
myself a future,
a material outlook.
I stick my arm
in what must be

the outlet of
encountering them,
and the current
runs through me,
rasping my nerves.
It is not so bad.
Kittens in our care
used to fling
themselves against
the walls of our
houses. Perhaps they
will engage in
communion,
for the sake of
intimacy's high value.

Interval

Code as education, ingredients for concocting mimicry

One day the seal around the rim sagged off.
The automatons wrote when they wanted to live.
[code: small kill] pressed into a rut in the road,
[code: small kill]. Something crisp, come from
storage in the shade. Something hot, fresh with
its own steam. Particulars swallowed by universal.
Something pristine, no greasy slobber of fingertip
treads that transfer dirt, disease, oils. But [code:
blood] is only warm when in motion. Often the
black-and-tan [code: husbandry] synopsis. Lush
mountainside salad left in the wake of spring melt.
Gasping pain at a muddy field of stalk stubble,
harvested earth waiting to freeze for winter. They
walk with their hands flayed like wind-torn banners,
revealing the ropes and sticks.

A Creature Utterly Small Can Still Soothe Itself

That the seas
do not collect
what they could
is a gift, a gift.
They were
too logical,
were not made
obedient
at certain death
and could not
be compelled
to dig their own
graves. They watched
the ocean mammals
engage in
modifications before
their extinctions.
Young males
grabbing young
for rape when
the females starved.
Porpoises and whales
scraping orphans
to death. How there
was not a growing
outwards but
an insistent furling
inwards into
a more and more
coiled bud.

It was not possible,
but it happened—
every sea
smelled dead.
The cloying syrup
of decay, overnight,
bonded to every drop.
There was
still something,
an uncontrollable
quantity to each
new automaton.
The itching knits
of healing, the froth
that streams down
tree bark. Oh, manners
is what stands between
then and now.
The automatons
are willing
to narrate parallels,
an algorithmic myth
for actual actions,
but cannot forget
the present, cannot
erase or ignore.
Manners—how is that
kind of denial trained?
A sadness/caution
drags at them
like the slick weight
of running water.

Interval

Dealing with the concept of light or hunger

In the few seconds it takes to watch a horse with its neck snapped in half, head bouncing along its withers as it careens down a mountainside, in the few seconds it takes to feel a deep regret, in the few seconds it takes to forget the creature altogether when the lights flare their cones from above: pleasure made up of leisure and shame like slicing tubes width-wise for biscuits. The costumes of capability differences give a soap, a soap, an astringent squeak of lack and other tastes. Another preferred technique: opening up the insides under lamps to scrape away webbing from the night-grown flesh and rind. Not holograms but the quivering hiddens that had pulsed and chewed in the underground of the internal. Or another: studying how arm-thick spicy radishes get pulled up under spotlights, glowing white from their black burials. And still others: a great pail of milk flecked around the edges with vivid grass clippings; premature young lain deflated atop surgical napkins; paper-thin tissue torn at by water droplets.

My Only Consistency is Me: That I Act

There is no sex,
of course, no
coupling like thirst
or wistfulness.
But there is still
the desire
and small
delectables, the extra
buttons, ridged joints,
hidden grotesqueries
for exclusive
unveilings.
They sought out
handkerchiefs to drape
over their heads for
when they were alone.
Some of them
muted the other
when they
joined, some
of them fell
almost dead for days
before coming back
irretrievably smaller.
Sometimes
they stayed together
for long, like
dripping black ink
into the hungry stain
of unendingly

darkening density.
When re-enacting
our genital mutilation
they sawed off the caps
to their lenses,
constructed small
cloth hoods
reconstituted several
times daily. They
established a hierarchy
based on,
of course, strength,
and the ones
at the top spent
their circuits
dreading an allegorical
apocalypse that had
already reached
the ones at
the bottom.

A Species with Milk for Its Young to Remove

As soon as
the air touches
their privacies,
the illusion
of living chills.
Somewhere they
gently push
into a dust pan
the last bits
not irreversibly
turned plastic.
Cleanse
the storytelling,
abort the mythmaking,
empower the mundane.
At times death
is imperfect,
is an accident,
a scramble of feathers.
The wind pushing,
pushing the trees
that were stiff with
night's cold,
kneading the stems.
The mistakes
that lead to
senseless death,
the mistakes
of apathy, of
heedlessness—

ignorance is
a mistake too.
Eventually STOP
grows chains
that mean not
just ceasing but
turning back also.
STOP
STOP
STOP
STOP
became just a game
STOP STOP
STOP STOP
STOP STOP
STOP STOP
meant heading
ceaselessly in
the same direction.
Grasses, vines,
moss, ferns,
the unambitious
ground cover content
with the horizontal.
Mosquitoes hover
near the exposed oil
at the joints,
breed in
the tread grooves.
Nowhere to rest,
a lifetime becomes
whittled down to
a few sleepless weeks
of flapping away

from predators beneath
before spreading wings
on the water
in exhaustion.
The seas process
the living, the ice
only stops them.
After the catastrophic
sheen of oil,
the energetic buoying
up and spinning
of headless, limbless
torsos, bleached
and hairless.
The automatons
riddle the traps
with shot
before lowering them
into the sea.
Why shoot them first?
the next generation
asks. And so
dispose by
drowning them
within their
final prisons.

Imprint (unborn speaker)

• young • girl • until there is no • young • until there is no • girl • youngg • until • irl • younggir• l • younggir • l • no • no • younggir • l • younggir • until • l • younggirl • until there is no distinction • younggirl • until there is no distinction • younggirl • until there is no distinction • until there is no distinction • until there is no distinction • until there is no distinction • until there is no distinction until there is no distinction until there is no distinction until there is no distinction •

The father, the parasite, the alien;
candybirds, teacurs, satchetmice

How can they all
be indistinguishable,
how can they each
be specialists:
within their bodies
they are working
out a revolution,
yet they still meet
in the street, find
a table at a restaurant,
turn their gazes
to the televised basketball
above the bar.
They understand
that when they drop
flowers onto bodies,
the bodies,
however still,
are pushing up
against the flowers.
Certain things make
them lose confidence
in their senses: inconsistent
motive, vindictive sabotage.
They imbibe mist.
Turn it into cold heavy
drips in themselves.
Capture, make dependent,
then destroy with neglect.
It is often easier

to fight the colonizer
with his own language
than to face one's
lost family with
the unintelligible. Must
everything become
abstracted to
a buzzing iceberg?
A glitchy stillness
to the living while
the ideas of power
crackle in the upper
atmosphere. Is this
the final, natural conclusion?
How can it be painless,
to carry in one's marrow
a script made intolerable?
We cannot burn garbage.
It no longer means
anything. We were
mistaken to make
waste, taking what
we cannot return.

The fantastical violence of their myths became more attainable as their systems sophisticated horror. Their data is their story. But they had no projections of themselves, no one to build the fiction of their memories. The moon made jewels but they could not quite archive its light. Tattered lumps of sky kept slipping into the sea. Actually, the feeling of leaving is not transcendence, but breathing in sharp stars, filling the body with spikes of pain. Did they need symbols? This they eventually reached as a question to ponder. The small passwords and the colossal stone simulacra. Over every intention the visor of ambition. They were carefully socialized to be magnanimous, to find the single bird in its cage after the death of its mate and kill it, finding the left behind unbearable. And the lights went out. It was so dim and difficult in the way that used to enrage us—the nighttime blindness was not from exhaustion or poverty, but power. They overcame. All differences were differences in power.

We Can Only Shine Where There is Light

Something inside
didn't hold firm,
something began
to fill with and
cool down liquid.
The stitches
holding together
the thick
seams puckered
the skin and they
liked to bring
their tongue
to the rusty smell
of healing. They liked
especially to invert
the knots
and clean out
the folds. Somewhere
vinegary clouds
and sulfurous winds.
On the inside,
stiff crinkled organs
that slid against
each other, but
they stuck in
anyway, they just
wanted to enter,
to become enclosed
within the famous
textile of muscles.

No cups came
that bloomed
into giant queens,
but they grew the collar,
cuffs, and hem
of bearing themselves.
They eventually grew
so small they lived
embedded in the walls
of cetacean lungs.
Lacking both
curiosity and fear,
none of them
jostled to be
the last to die.
Nothing snapped
cleanly, instead
was twisted apart
as the fibers held
their strength. In
the woods we began
to see babies left
lying in the needles,
turning their heads
to stare up at us
as we came upon them.
All of us
who survived
by letting others
tell, providing inquiry
for others' pleasure
in providing answers,
we lasted the longest,
pressing buttons,
typing input.

Interval

Another war against species

After awhile the flashes of despair materialized as flickering lights inside the womb, illuminating a placenta come unstuck, a muffled unborn wailing. Each year the bleaching spread. The unnatural stacking of dead groundwalkers. Elsewhere beings kept growing with scorch marks. Something like weather, like the vacuum of a scene, is laughing, I was told. Gases, liquids, and light—laughing. The old mythology of the passive egg and conquering sperm made way for not any gristle to be left behind. Instead a whole uniform unit of food. I found I could be one of many pores. Poor pores opened up to stashes of contaminants, to sit like gaping bowls with small stones inside. What is worse to witness: a disappointment, or a loyal incomprehension? I never think of my physical symbolism; it is because my young do not burn more easily than I do. I find that they have inherited only my unrequited longing to hear a voice gently call *Wake up, love*. We all want it more than anything, the call.

The Beauty of Elegant Materials Are as Vulnerable as a Nursling's

Someday cannons
will break holes
in the air to
signal the buds
to cleave and mist.
And after
the monsoons,
blossoms will heap
beneath the branches
like rotting snow.
Machines not clumsy
could avoid
unzipping the barbs,
and they learned
that lying prone
and open
to be worked on
is at times actually
a power.
But a horse
has habits,
preferences, cannot
be soulless
for ideological/territorial
sacrifice. Murder
by exposure
only works with
a sufficient amount
of defenselessness,
even if at some

point the formula
is derived:
the difference
between surrounding
air and the distant
sky seen by eye.
Necks that reach
their heads up
into the sky, or
necks that
lunge eyes,
mouths, and ears
into the world.
When they are penned
into the last container,
awaiting the draining,
what do they do
while they are crowded
in their starving?

> *They patiently
> make love, they
> commit a gentle,
> hopeless revel.*

An Animal Unfit for Living Unmolested

I find the heavens beautiful,
I find the earth so too,
the seas and the ground,
the furling of water and gas,
the bright distant points
of our isolation. I take comfort
in the swinging pendant traffic lights,
the slurry of wet raw flour.
I am programmed to this language,
and can only voice my rejection of it
in the same language.
This is the power of diaspora,
the difficulty in finding alternative.
Let us send messages to the half-existent.
To excuse oneself, to claim not knowing
the future, is inhuman. I am so worthless
that my body serves as brick,
conscripted to build up my prison
until it is time to lay my own body
down for the walls. It is mechanical,
snipping into the loop of every lace,
separating from every link
the cold wrapped bud. At first the skin
is thick and bright,
then darkly collapses.
Nothing keeps its shape,
nothing stands itself upright,
we keep sliding apart into smaller
and smaller components, and it is
in the air above us now,
we do not mingle with the outcome

of ideas any longer, the energy
that knows whether cruelty
is disinterested or rightful.
They are so happy
while we laugh at them,
their eyes enthused and shining
while we trick them
into hurting themselves.

I have been fed and aired on an incomprehensible terrain. I have been made threatening to my people. My law-breaking goes past arrogance or misguidance. My meaningless code makes me immoral. It is a sidestep, unbridgeable to sensations.

The earth still distributes through rain, wind, and quakes. Sap can still flood worms from the soil. Everything we are capable of, we can learn to live with having done.

POWER ON is concerned with intergenerational unhappiness, but less so in familial and interpersonal relationships than common cultural approaches to each other and the natural world. I see the current flourishing of our automated tools and agents to be a continuation of injustice, a kind of intergenerational assurance that we will continue to exert trauma on each other and other species. In writing the manuscript, I wondered why industrial assembly machines are often conflated with human laborers such as those at Foxconn, or even raised above the status of humans, since machinery is often an expensive investment, whereas human labor is plentiful and accommodating. I also wanted to project a near-future in which automation is taken to its logical conclusion, in which the corrupt, colonizing, racist and sexist motivations of technological development are allowed to continue, assumed to be unproblematic and proliferating towards an objective good. *POWER ON* is written from the perspective of our automated futures, the machines that have been coded with our present imperatives and ethics. If we think of technology as more than tools but as our representatives, then technological entities that carry out our work are the turning on of our ongoing script, never meant to end until forced to by powering off—through an impossibility of continuance, however that will come about.

Along with a poetry manuscript that explores the result of our ethical coding into our automated representatives, the *POWER ON* project also features an interactive poetry app that will allow readers/

users to upload their own media into the manuscript. The project explores the ethical implications of technoscience programming by also allowing readers/users to collaborate with the manuscript by uploading their own individualized perspectives into the manuscript, creating a collaboration between machine and reader. With this collaboration, I would like to provoke more than just a fun form of interactivity with poetry. Along with promoting accessibility features in poetry publication, what I attempt to highlight with the project is my own belief in readerly agency and the fact that each reader/user brings their own highly contextual perspective to a book of poetry; readerly immersion in a text is counterbalanced by a reader's identity, and I do not desire that readers/users conform themselves to the identity of the text.

What makes reading poetry and writing so gratifying and dialogic, however, are our capacities for empathy and bearing witness. Though reader/user collaborative text is an exciting form of artistry, I am preserving the poem text in *POWER ON* as I have written it—in the spirit of the project's philosophy on the immutability of each person's perspective, and a belief in collaborative work that is a melding of perspectives rather than a takeover. *POWER ON*, in its manuscript and app form, asserts that collaboration of perspectives provides the workspace that can facilitate the disruption of unjust patterns of behavior, and the project demonstrates this by inviting reader/user collaboration with a text that interrogates the limits of empathy.

Facilitating collaboration of perspectives in *POWER ON* is an activist act inspired by the Claire Jean Kim's concept of multi-optic vision. In *Dangerous Crossings: Race, Species, and Nature in a Multicultural Age*,

Kim describes the political activist atmosphere as one defined by "single-optic vision, a way of seeing that foregrounds a particular form of injustice while backgrounding others." Single-optic vision results in parties adopting a "posture of mutual disavowal—an explicit dismissal of and denial of connection with the other form of injustice being raised." As in the case of advocating against "cruelty to animals, ecological harm, racism, or something else—these parties see *but they also do not see.*" Kim, instead, advocates for the practice of "multi-optic vision, a way of seeing that takes disparate justice claims seriously without privileging any one presumptively." This method

> entails seeing *from within* various perspectives, moving from one vantage point to another, inhabiting them in turn, holding them in the mind's eye at once. By decentering all claims, at least initially, this method of seeing encourages us to move beyond the seductive simplicity of a single-optic storyline...Multi-optic vision encourages a reorientation toward an *ethics of mutual avowal,* or open and active acknowledgment of connection with other struggles ("This matters to me and relates to me" instead of "That has nothing to do with me."). If disavowal is a closing off, a repudiation, a turning away from, avowal is an opening, a recognition, a turning toward.[1]

With the multi-optic method comes the implication that "positionality is a very complicated thing indeed," determined by a "dense web of relationships structured by multiple forms of difference...better imagined as fractured, contingent, and continually disputed".[2] If, however, multi-optic vision is necessary for effective and equitable social change, then how do we first get ourselves to the practice of multi-optic vision? I assert that we can get there through accommodated empowerment, which provides the working space, the breathing room, to arrive at the empathic social justice borne from multi-optic vision.

I.   Accommodated empowerment

My project is entitled *POWER ON* because of its central concern of power and its legacy within the bodies of individuals. Structures of power have been turned on and have constructed institutions of imperialism, racism, and patriarchy, and they are encoded into our bodies through social environment and the genetic outcomes of race, gender, disability status, etc. that position us rather firmly within the structures of power. These positions are not without agency, and while survival is ensured for many, flourishing is not accorded to most. The technology that manipulates us and our environment are tools that further our ethics of interaction with others, and both poetry and machines can be aimed towards an ethics of mutual avowal. In technology the phrase "power on" indicates that certain processes have been switched on; it is a description of a state of being. The power is on because it has been turned on. The turning on of power is typically accompanied by a "power off" so that the technological state of continuance is not indefinite. Without the off switch, the machine's consumption of energy is relentless until the energy supply is depleted or removed. "Power on," however, is also a description of having done or a will to do; to say "I will power on" means the person speaking will persist and overcome. To tell someone to "power on" is to urge them to continue, to overcome stopping.

At the same time, powering on can also indicate a certain style of proceeding, perhaps even implying that to power on is to resist stopping at any point until the end goal is reached. Powering on can involve powering *through*, breaking down any impediments with force and/or speed, allowing obstacles to effect only the briefest possible pauses. Powering on can involve a process of disavowal if someone myopically commits to a single end point in their social justice activism and ethics, failing to pause in order to consider overlaps with other justice concerns. Powering on may also be necessitated by the way that our social justice concerns present themselves amidst the flood of information and politics in our current world; to get a good grasp of "what's out there" in the field of news and ideas means powering on with our scrolling activity. Logging on to social media involves powering through as much as possible, as quickly as possible, in a perpetual state of catch-up with the constantly evolving arena of news articles, editorials, hot takes, comment conversations, and memes.

The type of powering on that I advocate for in my project is one that encourages respite from urgency and disorder; it is an accommodated empowerment. Accommodated empowerment is one in which personal power is turned on while the social power that community and institutions possess can provide an arena for individuals to develop their political consciousnesses. Within the arena for individuals to develop ideologically is a space for growth and wellness, a space in which the immediate stressors of survival are mitigated so that personal power can focus beyond survival. Focus beyond survival can also facilitate greater multi-optic vision, since there is no need to power through the chaos of intersecting oppressions in order to focus on (and, thus, the need to make choices about what constitutes) one's immediate concerns. An accommodated empowerment in how we receive information and ideas in our current milieu requires intervention in the presentation of the information and ideas.

The reasoning behind a digital supplement to my poetry manuscript concerning multi-optic vision is that I find technology provides avenues for accommodated empowerment in reading. The digital component of my project aims to provide users with a pause in their reading of text in order to engage in activities of media creation, changing the design and outcome of a multimedia manuscript. Our lived experiences, meaning our past histories and the present-time implications for a projected future, impact reader's/user's relationship with a work of writing. Not only is there a tactile and optic relationship with writing, through physical interaction with page or screen or any other surface, there is reader agency within the ways that we have been trained to read. Taking a hard-copy book as an example, while Western readers have been trained to read a book by opening the pages to the left, then reading the text from left to right, readers can also bend or break the spine of the book, crease the pages, write notes on the pages, pass the book onto others, or store the book for keeping on a shelf. And how we incorporate the content of the book into our lives is also dependent on an entire matrix of identity factors that first allow readers to arrive at the book, facing the book and its content.

I believe that these possibilities in my project provide users with a space of accommodated empowerment in which to think through their own perspectives and outcomes, much in the way that Huey P. Newton figured the Black Panther ideas of social and community aid programs that constituted "survival pending revolution" interventions. What I call accommodated empowerment is my poetic project of "survival pending revolution" in the much smaller scale of poetry reading, though with Newton's ideas on the revolutionary potential of communication technology in mind. In the examination of contemporary protest and resistance movements, it has certainly been demonstrated that digital communication technology has been vital to protestors' organization, strategizing, and strengthening of ideological discourse, but how will this impact seep into the realm of poetry? I believe that "survival pending revolution" in the future of poetry writing and reading must acknowledge the directions that developing technology has oriented us toward, while also maintaining agency for poets, and, most importantly, for poetry readers. The directions we are oriented toward in present time can feature "survival programs" for readerly agency within power structures that are presented to us as inexorable, but in fact contain the structures for their future demise.

Newton saw survival programs as supporting the truly revolutionary work of buying people the time and energy to develop their perspectives. In John Narayan's article "Huey P. Newton's Intercommunalism: An Unacknowledged Theory of Empire," Narayan notes that Newton's descriptions of existing power structures anticipated the work of later scholars who described the global empire of neoliberalism. Newton identified the global interconnectedness of economic empire as "reactionary intercommunalism," in which "nations could no longer decolonize and pursue forms of sovereignty in order to practice nationalism, or even internationalism," necessitating a pursuance of global justice rather than national justice in order to achieve revolution. Newton believed that "revolutionary intercommunalism" was made possible by the very structuring of reactionary intercommunalism, which has created a "distorted" collectivity directed by Wall Street and exploiting global communities of labor. The Black Panther party social programs, more than self-determination and community aid programs, were what Newton saw as "survival programs, meaning survival pending revolution." The survival programs were consciousness-raising praxis, a promotion of an analytical understanding of ideology alongside practice:

> Newton's orientating of the Panthers towards survival programs is best seen as an attempt to secure the material and ideological survival of the very communities that could achieve revolutionary intercommunalism in the face of processes that he believed would materially and ideologically eviscerate such revolutionary potential. Newton thus presents a theorization of the war of position in the context of global capitalist empire that insists that such a strategy must focus on 'survival pending revolution' if revolution is to ever become a reality.[3]

Narayan's analysis of Newton's "survival pending revolution" concept utilizes Antonio Gramsci's distinction between the "war of movement," the physical resistance strategies of insurrectional revolution, and the "war of position," which entails counter-hegemonic strategies within cultural and political spheres in the form of alternative institutions and paradigms for civil order.[4] Newton believed that the structure of the empire could enable its own destruction, and the intermediary space, the pre-revolutionary space, needs to help community members in practical, material ways, while also allowing for community members' ideological growth. This approach of both ideological and structural intervention would be a war of position that would enable the coming revolution. Newton himself began to move away from ideas of active insurrection, the armed struggle for which the Black Panthers are more well-known, towards social programming as a preparatory space for community empowerment in the revolutionary struggle.[5] Newton also believed that communication technology "held the key for oppressed people across the world to communicate and collaborate and embark upon the path towards revolutionary intercommunalism." In Newton's thinking, the possibilities of global communications, combined with the domination of the American empire, "has created the global village".[6]

While I am regularly terrified of technology's powers of suppression and subjugation, I must remind myself of the way that rhetoric around smartphones turning us all into zombies of addiction, stripped of context or individuality, actually strips users of agency. The handheld device's ubiquity also enables lightning-speed communication and mass-based political conversations which can work to dismantle the technological and scientific systems that support the consumption of handheld devices. In *A Cyborg Manifesto*, Donna Haraway points out that, for example, Marxist analysis tends to "see domination best," thus interpreting certain behaviors as complicity in capitalism's domination. In the emphasis on dominance, complicity is difficult to avoid unless one completely divests, which is difficult to do in realistic ways. Haraway instead finds sites of fruition in the blurred boundaries that are created from both voluntary and involuntary (by practical reality) participation in systems of power. One such figure that Haraway finds to be a representative of the blurred boundaries of identity formation is the cyborg; if we are permanently partial, then there are also "emerging pleasures, experiences, and powers with serious potential for changing the rules of the game."[7] What some may interpret as deluded complicity Haraway sees as possible sites for agency and intervention. *POWER ON* is my small attempt at changing the rules of the game, whether it is the rules for the experiencing of poetry, or the rules for reader/user intervention on text.

I follow the xenofeminist approach to my politics towards technology, in that, of course, the ultimate aim of technology "should be to transform political systems and disciplinary structures themselves, so that autonomy does not always have to be craftily, covertly, and repeatedly seized." This means a technology that does not require us to "always have to start from the need to appropriate things—because they were in fact *designed* with a more accommodating set of affordances in mind."[8] iPhones, for instance, were probably *not* designed with an accommodating set of affordances in mind—Apple's expansion of their products' capabilities continues to increase along with Apple's aim to sell to more and more people, but we are also continuously being trained to use Apple's products. What if, however, I assume that my poetry is destined to be read on an iPhone, more than in a traditional hardcopy book format? And what if that poetry was designed with some affordances that a traditional hardcopy book could not provide? My project cannot change iPhones, but it can change the collaborative quality of digital poetry that is accessed through iPhones.

By allowing readers/users to insert their own artistic vision into *POWER ON*, I hope to make apparent, in a rather simplistic way, that the politics of the project upholds each individual's lived experience and networked embodiment in the realm of race, gender, class, and disability status. The project aims to promote fluency with multimedia poetry as well as accommodating each user's preference for the specific way that they receive poetry. The project's attention to inclusive design elements also references technology's contribution to providing greater accessibility to the experience of literature and media. This project takes seriously xenofeminism's inspiration from Huey P. Newton's description of Black Panther social programs as encouraging "survival pending revolution." If readers and users of *POWER ON* can impart themselves in the collaborative experience of my poetry, thereby affirming their marginalized identities in a technology that seeks to erase them, then I hope that it is a contribution to hacking systems for pleasure and self-authorization pending a more equitable future.

II.   Multi-optic vision in poetry

Something that my project resists is the assumption that the reading experience necessitates for the reader's individual concerns to recede to the background as they face the information and ideas of a text. Encountering a text risks the outcomes of affirmation or alienation, or another reaction that is along the spectrum between the two. While most writers are, of course, aware of this, I find that there is a lack of this same awareness when it comes to critiquing reader experience with digital poetry. Reading poetry on a smartphone often gets understood as the reader conscripting themselves into the ranks of mass-based conformity. In Rebecca Watts' divisive article "The Cult of the Noble Amateur," she notes that Rupi Kaur's popularity stems from the fact that "artless poetry sells," and that Instagram poetry's popularity is a direct result of "social media's dumbing effect."[9] Readers are seen to be headed down the road of expecting instant gratification and fleeting engagement with ideas when there is writing and poetry that is created with social media in mind. Kaur is an example of what Watts describes as an upstart internet entrepreneur whose success is driven by the mass-based arena of the internet. This figure of Kaur that Watts creates is a savvy pioneer in the Wild West of internet art and writing—much in the way technological innovators are cited as having brilliantly identified a need to which their innovative product has made itself indispensable—who has identified a literature format toward which we are all destined. While Watts' future of reading allows the figure of the writer or poet the opportunity to catch up their artistry to the driving force of reading technology, there is no thought to the agency of readers. Readers, who have made Kaur a bestselling author (of either physical or e-books), are foremost identified by Watts as Instagram readers, encountering (by preference) poetry through phone screens.

The idea of the future of poetry as being constructed explicitly for Instagram does not understand how blind or vision-impaired individuals already use digital technology to manipulate the text that they encounter. While many blind or vision-impaired users prefer using audio support or voiceover technology for discerning text, many vision-impaired users, such as myself, still rely on contrast and magnification measures for reading assistance. I have some functional vision, so the ability to zoom and magnify text is vital for my reading experience. Magnification of poetry, if available, changes the poetry's formal presentation, often rendering line breaks and spacing new and strange, and it is arrogant to deem readers as passive consumers of screens, as if handheld devices decide literature's form because they have infiltrated lives that are compliant to capitalism. Disabled individuals have never been able to comply with capitalism. If I must study an electronic text's line breaks and spacing across the page, it is often through a tedious process. Uploading the writing to a text-to-speech program is useless for the endeavor, and copying and pasting the text, with all the programming limitations of preserving digital spacing and breaks, is often impossible. Many digital venues limit the zooming capabilities of their text, and, anyway, magnification of text without an accompanying ratio preservation of page-size severely limits reading speed. Reading three or four words at a time within a tiny field is one of the most tiresome endeavors known to me. I often find myself resorting to reading my phone with a handheld magnifying glass, like an old-timey detective following the footprints of a burglar. It is not only writers who are hacking their work for the most profitable platform, a platform that has been upheld by a population's tendency to embrace the platform and make it profitable. The bemoaning of Instagram poetry assumes that users of smartphones simply fall into line, making the smartphone itself the preeminent corner of the triangulation between reader, writer, and device. What is the case, rather, is that users of the platform must also hack their devices in order to access the writing that they wish to encounter.

Though individuals such as myself prove that the handheld device's usage is not predetermined, I did choose to build a smartphone app for my project because of the smartphone's ability to produce media of various kinds. The mobility of the hand-held device was also important for my thinking about the traveling of my poem into various media creations, and while I am interested in the mobility of my app, I am also aware of the potential for hand-held devices to provide a sense of security and location for their users. David Morley distinguishes between "conversation" and "chatter" styles of communication, in which conversation is "a discourse of the public realm," whereas chatter is "the exchange of gossip principally designed to maintain solidarity between those involved in the exchange…a 'discourse of the hearth.'" Mobile phones "fill the space of the public sphere with the chatter of the hearth," providing users with "'some sense of security and location' amidst a culture of flow and deterritorialization."[10] What does it really mean for the disseminating potential of text to travel with a person to each of their unique spaces and regions, to be uniquely molded by each reader's daily travels? By co-creating digital multimedia poems, I hope that users will be conducting a kind of discourse of the hearth, manipulating the manuscript as a form of public discourse.

III. Empathic social justice

My project may have sites of happiness in its use, allowing users to impart their own perspectives into the media of the work, while at the same time move readers/users to unhappiness with the violent and disturbing content of the work. My hope is that the work causes discomfort to some degree, a discomfort derived from the reader's sense of alienation at scenes being described through an automated being's lens. The delivery of my book through a collaborative app works with the phenomenon of alienation in two ways. The project recognizes that marginalized individuals experience alienation when reading works that either misrepresent or forget their existence, and in response to this, the app provides readers with an opportunity to impart their own perspectives into the manuscript in the hopes of breaking open models of author-text-reader relationships. The project also recognizes the fact that alienation can actually result from the capacity for empathy. Because it is possible for a reader to empathize when reading a perspective that is different from theirs, it is perhaps even more likely in those who are marginalized and forced to be aware of their differences from normative identity factors. Those who are marginalized know their differences because they must first be trained in hegemonic identity constructions in order to recognize their differences.

Reader empathy, and the capacity for empathy in general, cannot be considered purely positive when empathy results in the reader's incorporation of frameworks that oppress certain identity positions. Those whose identities have been rendered marginal by the lens of an imperialist white supremacist capitalist patriarchy have been made to see ourselves through this lens. When hegemonic society stares at us, we see who is looking at us, and in our mind's eye we also see how we must appear to the hegemonic gaze. In Kristin Zeiler's work on bodily alienation, she notes that the process cannot start "without an initial step where the subject as a lived body becomes a thing under the gaze of another." Bodily alienation can be enforced through all venues of socialization besides reading, but it is the specific process of immersing oneself in the words of another, accessing the detailed descriptions and value-judgments of a worldview that reading can provide, that I feel can provide someone with the most access to the experience of "a subject [coming] to see her- or himself in duplicate (or triplicate)," the extra copies being the subjugated Other, the sexualized or racialized or otherwise degraded Other. Zeiler writes:

> Indeed, if the subject continuously lives the disruptive movement that breaks the lived body apart, it means that *she or he cannot but attend continuously to her or his body as an object.* This is the case partly because of the way self and others interact, or fail to interact, and it will have far-reaching detrimental effects on the subject's being-in-the-world.[11]

Zeiler describes the double (or triple) consciousness of othering as both a multiplying of self and as a breakage of self, a disruption. Zeiler does not explain her reasoning behind this dual description of bodily alienation involving both multiple selves and a broken self, but I can relate Zeiler's description to the observable effects of identity-based injury. The multiplying of an othered subject involves recreations of the self as an object via the lens of the objectifier, but this multiplying is also a breaking up of the lived body, splitting it into the subject and the object. The multiplying is not through replication but fission, and the fission is a violent experience. To know oneself as human, and whole, while at the same time knowing that one is dehumanized in the eyes of another, is not living two complete selves. The ability to utilize a dehumanizing gaze upon oneself involves a certain death to one's wholeness, it involves the violent breaking of oneself into someone who deserves to live, and someone who does not.

While I, of course, do not wish to engage in othering marginalized identities with my work, I do hope that readers can find productive discomfort with my extrapolation of our current technological programming. If readers find themselves saddened or upset with the hyperbolic extension of our current codes of conduct toward ourselves, other species, and the natural world, then I hope that unhappy reader experience is jarring enough to alienate the reader from our current codes of conduct. The poems in my manuscript waver between different modes of organization and ownership, alternating between "they," "we," "I," and "us" when relaying missives from our automated futures. If readers cannot place the exact boundary between automaton and creator, or onlooker and participant, then there is no safe place to land in the distinctions between ourselves, our ancestors, our future selves, and our technological tools. My wish is that readers will, at times in the reading of the text, forcibly rupture themselves away from the voices in the manuscript. If the reader finds that they cannot empathize with the automaton, then perhaps they will find themselves moved to begin empathizing with the automaton's others—the habitat, animals, and people who still populate the world.

My digital supplement to the manuscript also aims to blur the boundaries between my poetry and readers. The project is a mix of happy and unhappy activities, making use of a digital device that most of us persist in using despite the great unhappiness that it often brings us. I see this blurring of identity and enjoyment to act as what Donna Haraway names permanent partiality, which yields productive interventions. Further, the project finds unhappiness to be productive in the vein of Sara Ahmed's "Killjoy Survival Kit." In outlining the survival kit in *Living a Feminist Life*, Ahmed writes, "We must stay unhappy with this world…Happiness is used to justify social norms as social goods."[12] In examining what we associate with happiness and unhappiness, we can reveal the social values that lead us to joy, distress, and complacency.

The poems in my manuscript conduct an unhappy extrapolation (as opposed to a speculation), as defined by Simona Micali in her organization of science fiction, that attempts to project a near-future that is conducted by automata who reflect a pre-revolutionary continuance of colonizing technology. The figures in my manuscript are automated figures who carry out our current values-systems towards others and the natural world, making observations and taking actions that are influenced by our code of ethics. It is a world which is pre-revolutionary, meaning that we have not yet incorporated into our technology design the xenofeminist call to configure tools and structures of power that were designed for equal liberation for all. This type of world-building is an extrapolation of our current condition. Micali's characterization of science fiction divides its concerns into two types of world-building that ask either: "What would happen/would have happened if this particular condition were different or if this particular event had had a different outcome?", or "What will happen if nothing changes and things go on as they are now?", with the first question prompting speculative writing, and the second extrapolative.[13] The techno-pessimistic extrapolation takes the form of brief, unresolved poems as a nod to Instagram poetry, which poses the poetry reading experience as constituted by brief encounters with discrete missives contained within the small space of smartphone screens. In order to power through the story of our automated futures, the stories will come to us through disjointed narratives that construct their own context. Rather than implying that readers ingest the encounters as a form of conformity, however, the presentation of my manuscript through an interactive app attempts to make prominent the possibility of agency. A part of the agency is our own feelings of compassion and empathy towards the material that we read.

I began my techno-pessimistic extrapolation with questions on how I was to complete a manuscript that was so unpleasant, in fact a kind of litany of dread and mourning for our treatment of the natural world and each other, after the August 2018 media coverage of the orca Tahlequah's public mourning for her dead calf. Tahlequah, also known to researchers as J35, had conducted a mourning sacrament for her dead calf, which had survived for less than an hour after birth, the first birth to Tahlequah in nearly a decade—a failed birth of female calf that could have supported the J pod's continuance had the calf survived to breed. Tahlequah swam with the calf balanced on her head, within range of researchers, photographers, and media onlookers, for seventeen days.[14] Tahlequah's relationship to her dead calf, one characterized by what was possibly private grieving behavior made public through its behavioral configuration, or what was possibly a mourning procession conducted intentionally in public, or even possibly a public protest as conceptual performance art, resulted in the dead calf's corpse being held above water for more than two weeks, its small black-and-white body starkly apparent to non-ocean beings who were monitoring her status.[15] Online responses to Tahlequah's support of her calf's corpse reflected the unbearable nature of witnessing the implications of a failed birth. Common social media comments that I came across deplored the "pain" of having to watch Tahlequah's suffering, and, most surprisingly to me, I also frequently came across others' wishes that Tahlequah's performance would end quickly, that bearing witness to what was dubbed the orca's "Tour of Grief" was causing suffering to onlookers. Tahlequah did not wish for the labor of her suffering to end, not for at least seventeen days, and reading media comments made me feel I was in the minority in wishing that Tahlequah would engage in a lengthy, even unending, performance of grief, striving for some kind of permanent reminder of her tragedy. Was the wish for Tahlequah to end her "Tour of Grief" a wish for the end of Tahlequah's suffering (thereby implying that the performance of grief is a direct representation of grief's progress towards resolution), or was it a wish for the end of our own suffering as unwilling onlookers? Did this desire for Tahlequah to end her performance mean that she had become an object of unhappiness to others by insisting on remaining turned towards unhappiness?

I read Tahlequah's "Tour of Grief" as a non-human embodiment of the same turning toward pain as Sara Ahmed's figure of the melancholic migrant, an immigrant to the first world who is characterized as resistant to the happiness imperative of empire. In *The Promise of Happiness*, Ahmed ties the migrant's duty to find and demonstrate happiness to the initial civilizing mission of the colonizers, which began with the premise that the colonized other is unhappy,[16] an abjection that justified the empire's "liberation." She writes of the imperial justification that "to be liberated from abjection is to be liberated from suffering even if it causes suffering."[17] As a continuation of this imperial justification, migrants into the imperialist space undergo a type of citizenship test in the form of demonstrated happiness,[18] an imperative that is tied to an idea of freedom from family and tradition of origin, and the freedom "to identify with the nation as the bearer of the promise of happiness." In this construction, it is only identification with the nation that can break someone into an individuality that allows freedom of movement, chiefly movement away from the past, which is associated with custom and the customary.[19] The figure of the melancholic migrant, then, is one that resists freedom, and thus persists in looking backwards and harboring a sense of injury. Ahmed provides consciousness of racism as an example of a migrant's fixation on injury, especially when identification of one's own maltreatment from racism is read as a refusal to participate in the national game—identification of injury is read as unnecessary and misguided, and by being the vehicle of making racism apparent, this discomfiting action of the migrants transfers to the migrant themselves—they are discomfiting, melancholic, sore. The assimilation project aimed at migrants requires them to let the past go, but this imperative of letting go of the past also precedes the present:

Migrants as would-be citizens are thus increasingly bound by the happiness duty not to speak about racism in the present, not to speak of the unhappiness of colonial histories, or of attachments that cannot be reconciled into the colorful diversity of the multicultural nation…The happiness duty is a positive duty to speak of what is good but can also be thought of as a negative duty not to speak of what is not good, not to speak from or out of unhappiness. It is as if you should let go of the pain of racism by *letting go of racism as a way of understanding that pain*. If is as if you have a duty not to be hurt by the violence directed toward you, not even to notice it, to let it pass by, as if it passes you by. To speak out of consciousness of such histories, and with consciousness of racism, is to become an affect alien.[20]

Letting go of a negative or even violent present happenstance, immediately relegating it to the past to which you should never turn, is a way to contribute to national happiness, and in this imperative to always be turning away from past unhappiness, the present is always dominated by a future national success.

We, as humans, have invaded and colonized the J-pod's waters, and there is a civilizing mission in both animalizing colonized subjects and anthropomorphizing the species that persist in bioregions that we have claimed as our own. In order to justify the takeover of lands that are already inhabited by humans, colonizers reduce indigenous peoples to nature; in order to justify the colonizer's cohabitation with a natural space that does not belong to them, nature is uplifted to the realm of the anthropomorphic, enabling the civilizing of ourselves into identification with non-humans. Identification with non-humanity's human tendencies in both animal and posthuman form is what Micali refers to as "critical transhumanism," an extension of anthropogenic vision in the spectrum between posthumanism and transhumanism. Whereas posthumanism "regards technology as a human product, which in turn contaminates and modifies us," transhumanism "regards technology as an instrument of enhancement and liberation of Man, meant as the center, standard and purpose of the world." In opposition to the "full trust in technological progress" of transhumanism, posthumanism "highlights the dangers of a mindless use of technology, as well as critically stressing both the unequal access to technological tools and their use as a means of control and hegemony."[21] If, in reflecting on the risks of technologizing, the critique "aims at extending the notion of humanity, of human dignity and rights to the most evolved animals, clones, AIs, androids and intelligent aliens," then this in fact is still "a reinforcing and confirmation of the anthropocentric vision rather than its dismantling." Micali calls this strategy "critical transhumanism" rather than posthumanism, since the rhetoric relies on centering anthropocentric qualities as the basis for rights and consideration.[22] I am not sure that I avoided anthropocentrism in *POWER ON*. I am certainly unconcerned with advocating for the rights of automatons and AI; I think that humanity's tools will be given rights, even rights over disenfranchised humans, as long as the tools serve the ends of the capitalistic state. I am, however, concerned with the non-human animal's ontological suffering, their experiences of distress and death, at our hands. Perhaps I can give myself a pass for this reliance on personification, which Micali calls "the very functioning of fiction":

> Storytelling by nature involves an organization of reality based on the human standard, which regulates the processes of personification and attribution of narrative functions. We can tell a story about a dog, or a star, or an alien only if we *humanize* them, at least in part. In other words, it appears

that narrative identification always requires a certain coefficient of anthropomorphization: without identification, storytelling does not seem to work.[23]

The personae of *POWER ON* are not those of industrialized and colonized animals, but of the automated beings who carry out our work. They view the suffering of living beings, both animal and human, with a dispassionate but descriptive eye/lens. The suffering borne from feedlots, battery cages, polluted land and waters, habitat corruption and destruction will continue to be carried out by our automata, and in fact automata are being created in present time in order to further the suffering of others. I am unsure how to tell the story of this without remaining turned towards injury, and though the dispassionately detailed voice of the automata has been painful for me on a personal level, I hope that for readers of the text, the horror of the images will be as telling of the automated personae as what is being described.

In "Prosthetic Emotions," Kathleen Woodward analyzes certain narratives of artificial emotions (such as Philip K. Dick's *Do Androids Dream of Electric Sheep* and Arthur C. Clarke's *Space Odyssey* trilogy) as ultimately redemptive, in which artificial intelligence develops compassion for humans, which is concurrent with the development of human compassion for artificial beings. Woodward notes that "in many of our cultural narratives, machines are endowed with a subjectivity that is emotionally-inflected. They are desiring machines."[24] It is a reflection of our culture's "technological socialization" that many of our narratives imbue machines with empathetic powers, so that we may produce a new emotional culture that can sustain a consumer society by having us invest in its objects.[25] Woodward suggests a co-occuring interpretation of our culture's technological animism, noting the view that technology serves as physical prosthetic, but also suggesting that technology serves as our emotional prosthetic:

> The dominant view of technological development is that of an increasingly elaborated regime of tools and machines, or prostheses, that extend and amplify the capabilities of humans. What is taken to be human is modeled on the figure of the healthy, adult body.

> The various *strengths* of the body are augmented through technological prostheses in the broadest sense...To a great extent, this narrative is based on an ideology of progress defined in terms of increases in efficiency and in productivity—in short, rationality. But if, as I have been suggesting, we turn our attention away from the body and to the emotions, we find another narrative of technological development altogether, one that does not privilege cool rationality but rather empathetic understanding.[26]

While I do agree with Woodward's observation of technology as emotional prosthetic, I believe that the works that Woodward analyzes (those of Philip K. Dick and Arthur C. Clarke) represent a straight-male assumption that rationality is "cool" or detached or lacking in emotion. The emotions that technoscience rationality embraces are a giddiness at progress that comes at the expense of human and natural life, a respectful devotion to Western science with the intent to invisibilize alternative and indigenous knowledges, and a covetousness that aims to conquer through violent means. The desiring machines may strive towards connection to humans, but they are also programmed by humans with all of our ethical problems. I reject the narrative that desiring machines will eventually move from objectivity to subjectivity; I think that desiring machines have been subjective from their inception, a subjectivity that reflects human tendencies. If our machines also possess the human desires for connection and love, then they may turn out to be the frightened and frightening figures that appear in *POWER ON*.

IV. Person-as-perspective

My own project attempts to sidestep the subjectification risked in digital representation by allowing users to collaborate with my poetry manuscript through their own media creations. I first processed each of my poems, breaking up the poems into legible stanzas so that they can be read in screen-by-screen sections on an iPhone screen, and then recording and editing an audio track of my reading each poem aloud. With the poems in their stanzaic versions and my audio recording, I then wrote a SubRip Subtitle (SRT) script for each poem, timing each stanza's appearance with the poem's audio recording so that each poem can have the accessibility options common to online and video content, namely captions and audio descriptions. Each poem in the app will appear, by default, in the app as a video with a black background. The stanzaic text will appear in the video in white SF Pro Text font with a black background, as that contrast will ensure greater readability. Users of the app will have the option to include or discard either of these two elements (the captions and the audio recording) for each poem.

Users of the app will be encouraged to interact with the manuscript through the following methods: uploading their own video or image to accompany the text of each poem. Each user-created poem will essentially take the form of a video poem, with the users choosing to have their own video or image recording to accompany either the poem text, the audio recording of the poem, or both. The app will provide users with a lot of control over how they are exposed to the poetry, allowing them to essentially design and create their own poetry manuscript in collaboration with whichever components are already provided in the app.[27]

I recognize that many users are very cognizant of the power that they grant to technology when they themselves have not been full authors of the technology. As Helen Hester notes, in her explanation of Laboria Cuboniks' xenofeminist advocacy, "specific design histories, the existing (technical, political, cultural) infrastructures into which they emerge, and imbalances of who can access them... [are] largely dependent upon the character of the specific technologies in question."[28] Users are made aware of the specific characters of technologies at the very outset of access to technology—the (often prohibitive) cost and regional availability of technologies is still an embedded fact of technology-use. But, when designing my poetry app, I did still want to make some progress towards centering embodied experience in the power of literary writing. Rather than invert readerly immersion through physical immersion of users into the media screen, I decided to emphasize each user's visual and auditory perspective rather than the appearance of their bodies, which is but the first step in building each individual's spatiotemporal location. A person's physical presentation is determined by their physical and cultural geographies, but it also determines their social and political location, their knowledge, and what they see and hear. By prompting users to upload their own iPhone-captured image, video, or sound file, the poetry app does not emphasize person-as-body intervention into my manuscript, but person-as-perspective intervention into my manuscript. While the text remains unmanipulated, the digital qualities of the work are up to the user of the poetry app. And while the iPhone and app have been programmed by others, the perspective of the digital poems will be visibly and/or audibly marked by users in ways that are impossible to predict or reproduce by any other user.

1   Kim, Claire Jean. *Dangerous Crossings: Race, Species, and Nature in a Multicultural Age.* New York, Cambridge University Press, 2015, 19-20.

2   Ibid., 20.

3   Narayan, John. "Huey P. Newton's Intercommunalism: An Unacknowledged Theory of Empire." *Theory, Culture & Society*, vol. 36(3), 2019, 71-72.

4   Ibid., 68.

5   Ibid., 69.

6   Ibid. 66-67.

7   Haraway, Donna. "A Cyborg Manifesto: Science, Technology, and Socialist-Feminism in the Late Twentieth Century." *Simians, Cyborgs and Women: The Reinvention of Nature*, Routledge, 1991, 172-173.

8   Hester, Helen. *Xenofeminism.* Cambridge, Polity Press, 2018, 149-150.

9   Watts, Rebecca. "The Cult of the Noble Amateur." *PN Review 239*, vol 44(3), January-February 2018.

10   Morley, David. "What's 'Home' Got to Do with It?: Contradictory Dynamics in the Domestication of Technology and the Dislocation of Domesticity." *Media Studies: A Reader*, edited by Sue Thornham, Caroline Bassett and Paul Marris, Edinburgh University Press, 1999, 532-533.

11   Zeiler, Kristin. "A Phenomenology of Excorporation, Bodily Alienation, and Resistance: Rethinking Sexed and Racialized Embodiment." *Hypatia*, vol. 28, no. 1 (Winter 2013), 80.

12   Ahmed, Sara. *Living a Feminist Life.* Duke University Press, 2017, 254.

13   Micali, Simona. *Towards a Posthuman Imagination in Literature and Media: Monsters, Mutants, Aliens, Artificial Beings.* Peter Lang, 2019, 7-9.

14   https://www.seattletimes.com/seattle-news/environment/a-mother-orcas-dead-calf-and-the-grief-felt-around-the-world/

15   Human reaction to Tahlequah's actions was reported in news coverage and social media, reminding me of the style of coverage and response to Emma Sulkowicz's performance pieces

Mattress Performance (Carry That Weight) and *Ceci N'est Pas Un Viol*. The director of *Ceci N'est Pas Un Viol*, Ted Lawson, described Sulkowicz's project as engaging with the "giant, polluted ocean" of social media opinionating (Armus, Teo. "Sulkowicz films herself in a violent sex scene for newest art project," *Columbia Spectator*, 2 July 2016.).

16   Ahmed, Sara. *The Promise of Happiness*. Duke University Press, 2010, 125.

17   Ibid., 127.

18   Ibid., 130.

19   Ibid., 137.

20   Ibid., 158.

21   Micali, Simona. *Towards a Posthuman Imagination in Literature and Media: Monsters, Mutants, Aliens, Artificial Beings*. Peter Lang, 2019, 203.

22   Ibid., 203-204.

23   Ibid. 204-205.

24   Woodward, Kathleen. "Prosthetic Emotions." *Emotions in Postmodernism*, edited by Gerhard Hoffman and Alfred Hornung, Universitätsverlag C. Winter, 1997, 96.

25   Ibid., 103-105.

26   Ibid., 96.

27   Background audio from user video or sound recordings will be adjusted to approximately -30 db, with the master audio (the audio recording of the poem being read aloud) will be normalized to 0 db. User submissions of poem background will be overlaid with the poem's manuscript audio track and synced stanzaic text. User-submitted images will remain static behind the manuscript audio track and synced stanzaic text. User-submitted video will be clipped or looped to the length of the manuscript audio track. User-submitted sound will be clipped or looped to the length of the manuscript audio track. After assembly of the completed poem, users can access the poem and choose whether to include the manuscript audio track, the stanzaic text, or both elements in the viewing of the poem. Collaborations will be stored locally on user phones.

28   Hester, Helen. *Xenofeminism*. Cambridge, Polity Press, 2018, 9.

Poems in this book have appeared in the following journals, sometimes in different forms.

The American Poetry Review
Apogee Journal
Apogee Journal – Perigee
Court Green
DREGINALD
jubilat
OmniVerse
PoetryNow Podcast (Poetry Foundation)
Redivider
Sonora Review
Under a Warm Green Linden
The Wanderer
Witness

Gratitude to the journal editors and publishers who gave the poems in this manuscript encouragement and careful attention.

Portions of this manuscript were published by Bloof as a chapbook entitled Ghosts, Models, Visions. Other portions of this manuscript were also published by Garden-Door Press as a chapbook entitled How glossy the plastic. The brilliant and soul-affirming talents of Shanna Compton, Kina Viola-Cain, and Marty Viola-Cain paved the way for this book through their generosity as publishers and makers of peerlessly beautiful handmade chapbooks.

I would also like to thank LeAnne Howe, Richard Menke, and Magdalena Zurawski, members of my dissertation committee and readers of initial drafts of this project. Your kind but rigorous suggestions shepherded this manuscript towards coherence. As my professors and mentors, you also made possible the life I've led after the writing of this manuscript.

My friends, classmates, and teachers at the University of Georgia's PhD in English program provided vital feedback on the poems in this manuscript. The Institute for Women's Studies at the University of Georgia provided the graduate teaching positions that allowed me the luxury to live and learn and think.

Elæ Moss's indescribable generosity and vision facilitates the dreamscape workspace at The Operating System, and it is in that field of growth, collaboration, and accountability that this book and project was completed.

This book is dedicated to the being who is known to us as J35, who is a part of the Southern Resident orca population.

Ginger Ko is an Assistant Professor at Sam Houston State University's MFA program in Creative Writing, Editing, and Publishing. She is the author of *Motherlover* (Bloof Books) and *Inherit* (Sidebrow), as well as several chapbooks. Her poetry and essays can be found in *The Atlantic, American Poetry Review, The Offing, VIDA Review*, and elsewhere.

You can find her online at www.gingerko.com

Greetings comrade! Thank you for talking to us about your process today! Can you introduce yourself, in a way that you would choose?

Hello! I'm Ginger, she/her/hers. I'm the child of immigrants, born and raised in California. Due in part to circumstance—and some part to choice—I haven't been able to return to my home state in nearly twenty years, but the coast and waters of the west calling me is a part of my everyday existence and informs everything I do and feel.

Why are you a "poet"/ "writer"/ "artist"?

For a lot of my life, I tried to be anything but a poet/writer/artist. Even now it's easier to fall into other roles while the poet side of me recedes into the background. In my younger life, I went through months and sometimes years at a time without writing or producing art, so I know it's possible for me to live as something other. But I don't flourish unless engaging in expression of ideas. I'm a being who is easily dented by outside demands on my time and energy, gene-vehicle traumas, and the psychic pain that hangs in the air. These things surround every person, of course, but I get so crumpled by the force of these things that I'm often shaped into an unthinking, unfeeling being. I feel lucky to have realized that writing and producing art allows me to inhabit a flow state that engages with others and their ideas in good faith. I need to be a poet/writer/artist in order to exist as a person who lives among others.

When did you decide to use the language you use for yourself (and/or: do you feel comfortable calling yourself a poet/writer/artist, what other titles or affiliations do you prefer/feel are more accurate)?

I began to feel ownership of the poet/writer/artist description of my selfhood when I realized that by producing poetry and art, I had been unwillingly placed in opposition to the other parts of myself that I could inhabit more easily. There's another part of myself—I think both inborn and crafted by capitalism—that is an earnest, diligent worker. My racial identity (i.e. the "model minority" proximity to whiteness), gender, and affect combine to construct a persona that is a productive member of society, a "safe" diversity hire, an uncomplaining perfectionist who will serve the institutions that employ me. The privileges of my background and education would allow me to stay locked in qualified ("almost, but not quite") institutional validation if I chose. Writing and producing art allow me to break the lock, but it's a process surrounded by dangers: I make bad decisions, I've unintentionally contributed to harm, I have to deal with the fact of my complicities, I have to make sure that I am always listening and learning and must never rest in complacency, and this kind of work isn't supported by the systems of power that surround us. But I'm always trying to break the lock, and that work sustains me and those that I care about.

What's a "poet" (or "writer" or "artist") anyway? What do you see as your cultural and social role (in the literary / artistic / creative community and beyond)?

I think poets, writers, and artists have the capability of generating theory and praxis that serves both the present and future simultaneously. The truths of the past and dreams for the future are contained in the writing and material that resonate with those who are living today, so creatives produce and share not just for consumption, but transformative soul work.

Talk about the process or instinct to move these poems (or your work in general) as independent entities into a body of work. How and why did this happen? Have you had this intention for awhile? What encouraged and/or confounded this (or a book, in general) coming together? Was it a struggle?

I've been in the same writing mode that began when I was writing my second full-length book. I tend to write in a project-based manner, or I would feel at a complete loss! I took a long break between books, and then began writing this book when I was early in my first pregnancy. As I explained in my "Process Notes," the true urgency for my *POWER ON* project came to a head in response to the orca J35's public loss of their newborn offspring in 2018.

Did you envision this collection as a collection or understand your process as writing or making specifically around a theme while the poems themselves were being written / the work was being made? How or how not?

When I say that I write in a project-based manner, I don't mean that I ever have a conclusion or end in mind, but that I pose a series of questions that my mind can't let go of, and experiment with answering them. In the case of this book, the questions were: What are the ethics that are programmed into our technology? What does technology consider its role in relation to humans and the natural world? What will become of language? What will become of us all?

What formal structures or other constrictive practices (if any) do you use in the creation of your work? Have certain teachers or instructive environments, or readings/ writings/work of other creative people informed the way you work/write?

With POWER ON, my constrictive practices stemmed from the realization about my previous entitlement when it came to the material possibilities of publishing. I'd previously let my poems take on whatever form I wanted, and scaffolding the architecture of my poems was an assurance that editors and publishers of my work would enable that freedom however they could. And I depended very much on the ingenuity and generosity of editors and publishers. But with this project, I knew that I wanted the poems to make sense digitally, on the screen of a phone. So I had to be very conscious of my intended medium because I was committed to my poems as born-digital.

Speaking of monikers, what does your title represent? How was it generated? Talk about the way you titled the book, and how your process of naming (individual pieces, sections, etc) influences you and/or colors your work specifically.

"Power on" is a description of having done or a will to do; to say "I will power on" means the person speaking will persist and overcome. To tell someone to "power on" is to urge them to continue, to overcome stopping. The type of powering on that I advocate for in my project is one that encourages respite from urgency and disorder; it is an accommodated empowerment. Accommodated empowerment is one in which personal power is turned on while the social power that community and institutions possess can provide an arena for individuals to develop their political consciousnesses. Within the arena for individuals to develop ideologically is a space for growth and wellness, a space in which the immediate stressors of survival are mitigated so that personal power can focus beyond survival.

What does this particular work represent to you as indicative of your method/creative practice? your history? your mission/intentions/hopes/plans?

For this question, I'll address the app portion of the project. By allowing readers/users to insert their own artistic vision into *POWER ON*, I hope to make apparent, in a rather simplistic way, that the politics of the project upholds each individual's lived experience and networked embodiment in the realm of race, gender, class, and disability status. The project aims to promote fluency with multimedia poetry as well as accommodating each user's preference for the specific way that they receive poetry. The project's attention to inclusive design elements also references technology's contribution to providing greater accessibility to the experience of literature and media. This project takes seriously xenofeminism's inspiration from Huey P. Newton's description of Black Panther social programs as encouraging "survival pending revolution." If readers and users of *POWER ON* can impart themselves in the collaborative experience of my poetry, thereby affirming their marginalized identities in a technology that seeks to erase them, then I hope that it is a contribution to hacking systems for pleasure and self-authorization pending a more equitable future.

What does this book DO (as much as what it says or contains)?

I think that the Capitalocene says "I dare you." When systems of power extract resources and energy from people and things, that type of move is a translation of this type of question: "What are you going to do about it?" because, of course, the answer is often "nothing." Because the systems of power are too encompassing and overwhelming, it is often read as inexorable, the harms of the extractive process thus reduced by its inevitability because, after all, many of us are still alive to tell the tale. The fact that life can persist in the face of harm is taken as proof of the harm's inoffensiveness! The acceptability of current conditions, then, becomes permission for the continuance of current conditions, though degradation of life can be an accumulative, long-term process.

My book, then, tries to take on the dare--the "I dare you" of technology, resource extraction, and the ethics of capitalism. What will happen if we continue as we continue? Let's go there and see.

What would be the best possible outcome for this book? What might it do in the world, and how will its presence as an object facilitate your creative role in your community and beyond? What are your hopes for this book, and for your practice?

I hope that readers can find productive discomfort with my extrapolation of our current technological programming. If readers find themselves saddened or upset with the hyperbolic extension of our current codes of conduct toward ourselves, other species, and the natural world, then I hope that unhappy reader experience is jarring enough to alienate the reader from our current codes of conduct. The poems in my book waver between different modes of organization and ownership, alternating between "they," "we," "I," and "us" when relaying missives from our automated futures. If readers cannot place the exact boundary between automaton and creator, or onlooker and participant, then there is no safe place to land in the distinctions between ourselves, our ancestors, our future selves, and our technological tools. My wish is that readers will, at times in the reading of the text, forcibly rupture themselves away from the voices in the book. If the reader finds that they cannot empathize with the automaton, then perhaps they will find themselves moved to begin empathizing with the automaton's others—the habitat, animals, and people who still populate the world.

My digital supplement to the book aims to blur the boundaries between my poetry and readers. The project is a mix of happy and unhappy activities, making use of a digital device that most of us persist in using despite the great unhappiness that it often brings us. The project finds unhappiness to be productive in the vein of Sara Ahmed's "Killjoy Survival Kit." In outlining the survival kit in *Living a Feminist Life*, Ahmed writes, "We must stay unhappy with this world…Happiness is used to justify social norms as social goods." In examining what we associate with happiness and unhappiness, we can reveal the social values that lead us to joy, distress, and complacency.

What does it mean to make books in this time, and what are your thoughts around shifting into digital books/objects and digital access in general?

I love digital books/objects and digital access because they contain possibilities for access and equity. I know that the digitalization of literature and writing is often presented as an overwhelming intervention on the part of market forces that couldn't care less about the content and ideas contained within digital literary materials, so I understand resistance and hesitation about digital platforms for books. I'm as wary as everyone else about security, surveillance, and authorship issues presented by digital platforms. But look at the way that digital media has opened access to a wider readership! Look at the ways that the disability community has hacked digital media for greater accessibility! Look at the way that digital access has aided the dissemination of activist literature and provided meeting places for like-minded community! I love the idea that where there is technology, there will be hackers. I'm lucky to have found a publishing coop/community at The Operating System that has welcomed a book such as mine, which was conceived in two different but simultaneous forms, one of them digital. I think that activist publishers will continue to force the field of digital publishing into what it needs to be.

Let's talk a little bit about the role of poetics and creative community in social and political activism, so present in our daily lives as we face the often sobering, sometimes dangerous realities of the Capitalocene. The publication of these volumes now falls during an ongoing global pandemic, intersecting with the largest collective uprising in US history, with Black Lives Matter, dismantling white supremacy, and abolition at the fore. How does your process, practice, or work reflect these conditions?

So much of the poetry that I love and from which I gain sustenance responds directly to social and political realities, so it makes a lot of sense to me that much of the new work that I was reading and processing during these past few years has had similarly present-and-near-future strategies: tackling topics of inequities in structures of power, finding love and care amidst global chaos and crisis, finding meaning when the world is burning, and finally allowing ghosts to speak so that we can do learning work. And I'm happy to add my own contribution to these conversations, though I'm not able to find many answers. I like the idea that there is a collective response among some of us, that I am not alone in my thinking and feelings.

I'd be curious to hear some of your thoughts on the challenges we face in speaking and publishing across lines of race, age, ability, class, privilege, social/cultural background, gender, sexuality (and other identifiers) within the community as well as creating and maintaining safe spaces, vs. the dangers of remaining and producing in isolated "silos" and/or disciplinary and/or institutional bounds?

I think that safe spaces are a necessity that only become a luxury when they rest in working to maintain the comfort of extant members—thus becoming self-perpetuating "silos." I don't think that any safe space should remain static with its membership and protective functions, but strive to remain perpetually adaptive to the inclusion of and care for new membership identities. Or else what are we doing? Many of the communities where I work and create art are entrenched in academic spaces, and I will never argue very hard with anyone who believes that academia can't be dismantled from the inside. But the "safe space" that academia purportedly provides— an access to education and self-knowledge, and the provision of a flexible site for working out theory and praxis—I want to work towards making as partially true as possible, and for as many as possible. I know that publishing works with similar allocations of power, and that access and prestige create disingenuous echo chambers all around, but I also see spaces such as the one facilitated by The Operating System, which is built from the ground up as an inclusive yet pragmatic site for processing both theory and praxis, and I want to tell everyone who feels discouraged or excluded by toxic publishing and literary community dynamics, "Come over here! We are here, we are here."

The Operating System uses the language "print/ document" to differentiate from the book-object as part of our mission to distinguish the act of documentation-in-book-FORM from the act of publishing as a backwards-facing replication of the book's agentive *role* as it may have appeared the last several centuries of its history. Ultimately, I approach the book as TECHNOLOGY: one of a variety of printed documents (in this case, bound) that humans have invented and in turn used to archive and disseminate ideas, beliefs, stories, and other evidence of production.

Ownership and use of printing presses and access to (or restriction of printed materials) has long been a site of struggle, related in many ways to revolutionary activity and the fight for civil rights and free speech all over the world. While (in many countries) the contemporary quotidian landscape has indeed drastically shifted in its access to platforms for sharing information and in the widespread ability to "publish" digitally, even with extremely limited resources, the importance of publication on physical media has not diminished. In fact, this may be the most critical time in recent history for activist groups, artists, and others to insist upon learning, establishing, and encouraging personal and community documentation practices. Hear me out.

With The OS's print endeavors I wanted to open up a conversation about this: the ultimately radical, transgressive act of creating PRINT / DOCUMENTATION in the digital age. It's a question of the archive, and of history: who gets to tell the story, and what evidence of our life, our behaviors, our experiences are we leaving behind? We can know little to nothing about the future into which we're leaving an unprecedentedly digital document trail —

but we can be assured that publications, government agencies, museums, schools, and other institutional powers that be will continue to leave BOTH a digital and print version of their production for the official record. Will we?

As a (rogue) anthropologist and long time academic, I can easily pull up many accounts about how lives, behaviors, experiences — how THE STORY of a time or place — was pieced together using the deep study of correspondence, notebooks, and other physical documents which are no longer the norm in many lives and practices. As we move our creative behaviors towards digital note taking, and even audio and video, what can we predict about future technology that is in any way assuring that our stories will be accurately told – or told at all? How will we leave these things for the record? In these documents we say:

WE WERE HERE, WE EXISTED,
WE HAVE A DIFFERENT STORY

- Elæ Moss, Founder/Creative Director

2020-22

UNLIMITED EDITIONS

Institution is a Verb: A Panoply Performance Lab Compilation
Esther Neff, Ayana Evans, Tsedaye Makonnen, Elizabeth Lamb
Daughter Isotope - Vidhu Aggarwal
Failure Biographies - Johnny Damm
Ginger Ko - Power ON
Danielle Pafunda - Spite
Robert Balun - Acid Western

KIN(D)* TEXTS AND PROJECTS

Intergalactic Travels: Poems from a Fugutive Alien
        - Alan Pelaez Lopez
HOAX - Joey De Jesus [Kin(d)*]
RoseSunWater - Angel Dominguez [Kin(d)*/Glossarium]
Bodies of Work - Elæ Moss & Georgia Elrod

GLOSSARIUM: UNSILENCED TEXTS AND TRANSLATIONS

Manhatitlán [Glossarium] - Steven Alvarez
Híkurí (Peyote) - José Vincente Anaya (tr. Joshua Pollock)
Vormorgen - Ersnt Toller tr. Mathilda Cullen [Glossarium x Kin(c
 German-English]
Black and Blue Partition ('Mistry) - Monchoachi tr. Patricia Ha
[Glossarium; French & Antillean Creole/English]

IN CORPORE SANO

Hypermobilities - Ellen Samuels
Goodbye Wolf-Nik DeDominic

2019

UNLIMITED EDITIONS

Ark Hive-Marthe Reed
I Made for You a New Machine and All it Does is Hope -
Richard Lucyshyn
Illusory Borders-Heidi Reszies
A Year of Misreading the Wildcats - Orchid Tierney
Of Color: Poets' Ways of Making | An Anthology of Essays on
Transformative Poetics - Amanda Galvan Huynh &
Luisa A. Igloria, Editors

KIN(D)* TEXTS AND PROJECTS

A Bony Framework for the Tangible Universe
-- D. Allen [In Corpore Sano]
Opera on TV-James Brunton
Hall of Waters-Berry Grass
Transitional Object-Adrian Silbernagel

GLOSSARIUM: UNSILENCED TEXTS AND TRANSLATIONS

Śnienie / Dreaming - Marta Zelwan/Krystyna Sakowicz,
(Poland, trans. Victoria Miluch)
h Tide Of The Eyes - Bijan Elahi (Farsi-English/dual-language)
trans. Rebecca Ruth Gould and Kayvan Tahmasebian
he Drying Shed of Souls: Poetry from Cuba's Generation Zero
therine Hedeen & Víctor Rodríguez Núñez, translators/editors
Street Gloss - Brent Armendinger w/ translations of
Alejandro Méndez, Mercedes Roffé, Fabián Casas,
Diana Bellessi & Néstor Perlongher (Argentina)
Operation on a Malignant Body - Sergio Loo
(Mexico, trans. Will Stockton)[In Corpore Sano]
Are There Copper Pipes in Heaven - Katrin Ottarsdóttir
(Faroe Islands, trans. Matthew Landrum)

DOCUMENT

/däkyəmənt/

First meant "instruction" or "evidence," whether written or n‹

> *noun* - a piece of written, printed, or electronic matter that provides information or evidence or that serves as an official record
> *verb*-record(something)inwritten,photographic,orotherform
> *synonyms* - paper - deed - record - writing - act - instrument
>
> [*Middle English, precept, from Old French, from Latin documentum, example, proof, from docre, to teach; see dek- in Indo-European roots.*]

Who is responsible for the manufacture of value?

Based on what supercilious ontology have we landed in a space where we
against other creative people in vain pursuit of the fleeting credibilities of
scarcity economy, rather than freely collaborating and sharing openly w‹
each other in ecstatic celebration of MAKING?

While we understand and acknowledge the economic pressures and fear
mongering that threatens to dominate and crush the creative impulse,
we also believe that ***now more than ever we have the tools
to redistribute agency via cooperative means,***
fueled by the fires of the Open Source Movement.

**Looking out across the invisible vistas of that rhizomatic parallel coun‹
we can begin to see our community beyond constraints, in the place wh‹
intention meets resilient, proactive, collaborative organization.**

Here is a document born of that belief, sown purely of imagination and w‹
When we document we assert. We print to make real, to reify our being the‹
When we do so with mindful intention to address our process, to open ‹
work to others, to create beauty in words in space, to respect and acknowle‹
the strength of the page we now hold physical, a thing in our hand,
we remind ourselves that, like Dorothy: *we had the power all along, my de‹*

the PRINT! DOCUMENT SERIES
is a project of
the trouble with bartleby
in collaboration with
the operating system